PRAISE FOR BOOKS
BY JANE MARLA ROBBINS

MYASTHENIA GRAVIS: THE MUSICAL!
My Medical, Hysterical, Poetical,
Comical, 25-Month Memoir

"Myasthenia gravis attacked Jane Marla Robbins, and in this book she launches a brilliant counterattack. Her weapons, that embrace and actually suffocate it, are: wit, humor, word play, music, and yes, JOY."
– Jimmy Roberts, composer, *I Love You, You're Perfect, Now Change*

"Moving.... The book succeeds in capturing the manifold nature of illness, the way a sufferer can go from laughing to crying and back in a single moment. Jane's stay in the hospital is indeed nightmarish, as she is beset by giant birds, nurses dancing the cancan, and human-sized pill bottles screaming 'eat me.'"
– *Kirkus Review*

"As a physician and patient myself with Myasthenia gravis, I have to thank Jane Marla Robbins for making me laugh out loud about my own condition. It's what we all needed – deep-throated anger, belly-aching laughter, tears of tenderness, and hope for cures."
– Dr. Lisa Plymate, internist and geriatrician, living with MG for six years

"A wild, intense, wacky, honest, and wonderfully irreverent ride. This book has it all: the inanities and insanities of the American medical system; the grace and craft of good writing; and inspiration. A surreal and deeply insightful treasure."

– Jim Burroughs, Academy Award Nominee, Best Documentary Feature, *La Belle Epoque*; Academy Award of Merit, Documentary Feature, *Against Wind and Tide*

"Jane Marla Robbins makes you crack a smile and then she cracks your heart open, and then you laugh out loud again, and you can't stop reading."

– Bonnie Loren, actor, director, founder, Process Studio Theatre

"Two Beatles and a BeeGee walk into a bar. They see me. I say, 'Ya gotta read this book. It's outrageous, it's funny, it's heartbreaking. It's intelligent, it's important. It's music.'"

– Al Corley, film director, *Last Dance*; producer, *The Ice Road*

"Jane Marla Robbins courageously leads us into her whimsical, and deeply profound journey into her life with Myasthenia gravis."

– Kellee White, psychotherapist, spiritual medium

"Jane Marla Robbins writes about her travails with humor, elan, and a spunky defiance. MG may have impaired some of the author's vision, but not the most important kind: insight that opens new worlds to the reader."

– Liza Lee, School Head and Board Member: Hockaday School; Porter Gaud School; Columbus School for Girls

"Jane Marla Robbins brings her remarkable arsenal of humorous and heartfelt weapons to bear in her no-holds-

barred assault against an unpredictable foe. No matter how mad-cap and maddening the struggle might be, she always allows the reader a chance to recuperate and reflect. This is a deeply honest story about our shared human experience."
  – Peter Kazaras, Distinguished Professor of Music, Director of Opera UCLA, the UCLA Herb Alpert School of Music; opera stage director

ACTING TECHNIQUES FOR EVERYDAY LIFE
Look and Feel Self-Confident
in Difficult Real-Life Situations

"As an educator, former media and film executive and producer, I think Jane Marla Robbins has developed a fabulous confidence-building tool for people from all walks of life. What an idea! This book is a classic of the self-help genre and a masterful example of the power of a great teacher."
  – Stephen R. Greenwald, president, Metropolitan College of New York

"The techniques Jane describes with such insight, depth, and humor, are certainly veritable skills for success."
  – Adele Schelle, author, *Skills for Success*

THE TOPANGA POEMS

"A remarkable poem-log."
  – W.S. Merwin, United States Poet Laureate 1952, 2010; Pulitzer Prize, 1971, 2009; author, *The River Sound; Some Spanish Ballads; The Essential W.S. Merwin*

DOGS IN TOPANGA
2000-2018

"Evocative, charming, touching, insightful. And haunting. I laugh at one, cry at another. I couldn't stop reading."
  – Jack Grapes, author, *Method Writing, Any Style*

"Dog medicine for the soul."
  – Harry Hart-Browne, actor/playwright, *Special Delivery*

"Jane Marla Robbins has a keen eye for moments of beauty, and a wicked sense of humor....Pure Magic."
  – Hope Edelman, author, *Motherless Daughters; The Possibility of Everything*

POEMS OF COVID 19
Stuck in Lockdown: The First Three Months

"Bittersweet, funny and heartbreaking at once, a testament to our time. At times euphoric, at times sad, a haunting and tender tribute to her friends, as she celebrates and mourns them. A diary full of wonder, a hymn to life, and an uplifting meditation on loss, love and intimate tenderness."
  – Hélène Cardona, author, *Life in Suspension*, International Press Award, Best Book Award

"Some beautiful words to help take on an ugly time. Rage on, Ms. Robbins!"
  – Hank Rosenfeld, NPR

POEMS OF THE LAUGHING BUDDHA

"The great thing about Jane Marla Robbins is she conclusively proves that wisdom can be funny."
   – David Finkle, critic, *The New York Times Book Review*, author, *People Tell Me Things; The Man with the Overcoat*

"Lucky Buddha to find a home in Jane Marla Robbins' Topanga Canyon Garden, and have her take down his every wise word. Her poems will set you smiling, then laughing, then seeing, then smiling a deeper kind of smile. Step into her garden and make your day."
   – John Guare, playwright, Pulitzer Prize Finalist, *House of Blue Leaves; Six Degrees of Separation*

"In these brightly lit and joy-filled poems, all inspired by a stone statue of the Laughing Buddha, Jane Marla Robbins practically dares the universe to bring her down, and it cannot do so. In poem, after poem, laughter triumphs over whatever comes her way, and it is a literate, knowing laughter."
   – Gail Wronsky, poet, *Dying for Beauty,* finalist, Western Arts Federation Poetry Prize; *Blue Shadow Behind Everything Dazzling*

CAFÉ MIMOSA
IN TOPANGA

"*Café Mimosa in Topanga* is a lively, elegiac dance, full of love and healing."
   – Aram Saroyan, poet, *Complete Minimal Poems*, William Carlos Williams Award, *Day and Night: Bolinas*

ALSO BY JANE MARLA ROBBINS

POETRY

Poems of Covid 19
The First Three Months

Dogs in Topanga
2000-2018

Poems of the Laughing Buddha

Café Mimosa in Topanga

The Topanga Poems:
Fifteen Years in the Canyon

SELF-HELP

Acting Techniques for Everyday Life
Look and Feel Self-Confident in
Difficult Real-Life Situations

Perform at Your Best:
Acting Techniques for Business,
Social and Personal Success

DEDICATION

To and for my fellow Myasthenia gravis warriors,
the doctors who try to help us find ways towards
Glorious Remission, and the doctors and scientists
who will figure out a cure.

CONTENTS

Part II. POEMS, PRAYERS AND HEALING
The Next Seven Months,
April, 2021 – October, 2022

Part III. POEMS, RANTS AND HOPE
The Next Seven Months,
November, 2022 – May, 2023

Part IV. MARTHA GRAHAM, INITIALS MG

Part V. DID THEY REALLY HAVE TO ADD THE "GRAVIS??"

Part VI. FINAL SONG
After 25 Months, and Feeling Much Better.
November 2, 2023 (My Real Birthday)

FOREWORD

I wish this book were a roadmap for others with Myasthenia gravis, to lead them towards perfect healing. But Myasthenia gravis is a "snowflake disease," which means no two cases are alike. So there is no guarantee that what might work for me will work for anybody else. Instead, the book is an honest retelling of my own MG adventures, sometimes hilarious, sometimes not so funny.

It is a comfort to me that people with MG, and other illnesses, tell me that reading this book has made them feel better. Possibly less alone. As if this book were a warm blanket. Believe me, with what I know of MG, those who have it need one.

Over sixty-five thousand people in America suffer from Myasthenia gravis. It's been around for almost a hundred years, and there's still no cure. Nevertheless, in the twenty-five months since my diagnosis, my worst symptoms have disappeared, and I am beginning to live a more "normal" life. (Not that my life was ever that "normal" before.)

Also good news is that considerable and even promising research continues, and maybe, by the time you read this, a cure for Myasthenia gravis will have been found. I hope so.

May this book amuse you, open your heart, and even expand your understanding of the strange, complicated world of health and illness in which we live. Certainly, MG has done this for me.

Jane Marla Robbins
October, 2023

Part I. MYASTHENIA GRAVIS:
THE MUSICAL!
The First Seven Months, A Lunatic Outline,
September, 2021 – March, 2022

MYASTHENIA GRAVIS: THE MUSICAL!
The First Seven Months, A Lunatic Outline,
September, 2021 – March, 2022

PROLOGUE

The curtain rises to reveal a large screen hanging mid-air above the middle of the stage. On it the words "AUTO-IMMUNE DISEASE." In the middle of the stage, JANE, confused, slightly manic, sits at the wheel of a bright blue MG convertible, a bright pink patch over one eye, her blouse the same color.

JANE: The "AUTO" in question is not a Ford. Or a Volvo. Though its initials are MG – but not for some fancy sports car. *(A line of shiny cars drives across the stage.)* But for – "MYASTHENIA GRAVIS."

"Auto-immune?"
Immune to AUTOS, no, not I!
It's just hard to drive with a patch on one eye!

(Singing.) I've loved my cars,
They've had their scratches,
But this trip's different. This car crashes,

The diagnosis doesn't thrill me.
The good news is: it may not kill me.

I'm not "immune" to good ice cream,
And I've been known to eat my pints,
I'm not "immune" to love affairs,
(My heart's been broken more than thrice).

(Takes off her patch. Sings. To the tune of "I Feel Pretty.")

I see double. Double, double!
I feel stupid, and silly and scared,
Yes it's trouble:
I was definitely unprepared.

I see faces, like Picasso's,
With two noses and maybe three eyes.
Or they're blurry; and I worry
That nobody can tell me why.

(Speaking.) "Myasthenia gravis?" They had to add the
"Gravis?" It didn't sound serious enough?

I wear a patch, I don't see double.
Pink or blue, it's hardly trouble.

I really shouldn't drive a car.
'Cause I can't see what's near! Or far!

(JANE's head drops to her chest. With great effort she lifts it with her hand. She lets go. It falls again. Then she holds it in place with her fist under her chin.)

"Hold your head up high," my mother always said.

(Unhinged.) My neck....it won't hold up my head!

(A long-necked GIRAFFE ambles across the stage, neck and head slowly slumping. JANE'S fist releases her chin, her head plummets. Cymbals Crash.)

BLACKOUT

ACT ONE

SCENE 1. ON THE SCREEN:
"IN THE HOSPITAL.
Two Months Later"

(JANE lies almost propped up in a hospital bed, in a hospital gown, a purple patch on one eye. Around her are DOCTORS, ruby-studded stethoscopes around their necks, tap dancing.)

DOCTOR #1: *(Shuffles papers.)* It's Myasthenia gravis. *(Sees the patient.)* Oops, I see her name's not Travis.

DOCTOR #2: *(Reading.)* No, it's "Jane." Sees double.

DOCTOR #1: Can't move her arms or hands. That's trouble.

JANE: My neck is weak and I cannot chew.

DOCTOR #2: Not really sure what we should do.

DOCTOR #3: Any ideas for what direction we could go?

DOCTORS: *(Singing. Tune: "Be a Clown, Be a Clown, Be a Clown." Vaudeville hands.)*
We don't know, we don't know, we don't know....

JANE: *(Through gritted teeth.)* I'd rather have some escargots.

(Frustrated.) I'm missing real communication.
As if the doctors feared some litigation.

DOCTOR #1: *(Under his breath.)* What I need is a vacation.

DOCTOR #3: Though your disease is nothing new,
We just do not know what to do.

DOCTOR #1: *(Throwing up his arms, at a loss.)*
Give her everything. And quick!
Hope something here will do the trick!

DOCTORS: *(Singing, shoes tapping.)*
Try some Mestinon! Prednisone! Antibiotics!
Try steroids! And Batrin! Or try probiotics!

JANE: Like throwing spaghetti at a wall.
Oh, for a bowl of spaghetti – EXCEPT I CAN'T CHEW.

(A CLOWN enters, dumps a bowl of spaghetti, with tomato sauce, on her head. She pushes sauce into her mouth.)

I'm covered in sauce,
I feel like a jerk.
At least I can swallow.
I guess that's a perk.

BLACKOUT

SCENE 2. ON THE SCREEN: "UNDERSTANDING THE DISEASE"

JANE: *(Cross-legged on her hospital bed, in an oval of light, a green patch over one eye. In an exaggeratedly fake-smiling voice.)*

Messages can't get from my nerves to my muscles. If my nerves want to tell my eye muscles to "see single," the muscles never get the message. The lines are down.

(On the Screen: A deeply frazzled telephone operator, at her switchboard, Lily Tomlin's ERNESTINE from "Laugh-In," desperately, hopelessly tries to connect something to anything. Fails. And then she's gone. JANE, desperate herself, continues:)

So my muscles don't get their messages: to see single, or open my fingers and lift up my arms, so I could shake someone's hand, or *(Near tears.)* hug them.

It's as if, in your house, all the electricity were off, and you had no wifi, no lights, no oven. If it were Thanksgiving, you couldn't cook a turkey.

(A human-sized TURKEY shrieks across the stage.)

BLACKOUT

SCENE 3. ON THE SCREEN:
"THE DOCTORS"

(JANE, in a hospital wheelchair, yellow patch, three DOCTORS with her.)

DOCTOR #1: Jane, how many of me do you see?

JANE: I see two. Of you.

DOCTOR #1: *(Thinks he's witty.)* "The more the merrier."

JANE: *(More gritted teeth.)* But where's my terrier? *(Focusing.)* Where's my doctor?!

DOCTORS: Your doctor sent us.

JANE: Maybe this is a dream. Nightmare, more likely. These doctors don't know me. They're even unsightly.

Tweedle Dumb and Tweedle Dee.
No one knows what to give to me.

DOCTORS: There seems to be no cure in view.
For what to do: we have no CLUE!

DOCTOR #2: Where's a real Sherlock Holmes when we need one?! *(A line of determined SHERLOCK HOLMES*

DOCTORS, *giant magnifying glasses in front of their faces,*
marches across the stage. To "God Save the Queen.")

SHERLOCK HOLMES DOCTORS:
We don't have a clue.
And the woman can't chew.

(And they're gone.)

DOCTOR #2: Is there ever enough research?

DOCTOR #1: NEVER!

DOCTOR #2: We need more!

DOCTOR #3: MORE!

DOCTOR #1: NEVER!

DOCTOR #3: MORE!

A RAVEN: *(Flying through the air. Squawking.)*
NEVERMORE! NEVERMO'!

DOCTOR #1: *(As if his knowing this were clever.)*
That's Edgar Allen Po'.

JANE: I don't care that ravens mate for life.

JANE: *(Continuing.)*
Chewing's so hard I can only eat mush,
My walking's so wobbly, I fall on my tush.

(She tries to stand, falls. Cymbals Crash. Doctor #3 helps her up.)

DOCTOR #2: *(A rap artist.)*
I'm weary, I'm bleary, the hospital's dreary.
Let out what I'm feeling: I'm reeling.
But dealing!

I'm hardly inspired, I'm tired,
I don't wanna get fired.
People cryin', fryin', and dyin'.
Ain't no denyin' life is hard:
Gotta be a doc, take stock,
show cock, be a rock.
Here's the shock: I'm only human.

(He collapses into a final exhausted heap.)

BLACKOUT

SCENE 4. ON THE SCREEN: "LATE!"

JANE: *(In her hospital bed, frustrated. Polka-dot patch.)*
How long must I wait?! They promised the sheet.
I'm hungry. I'm starving. I'm dying to eat.

(She rings a loud buzzer. Nobody comes. She rings again. Nobody. She rings again. And again, the buzzers announcing the music from the song ahead.)

NURSES: *(Running in, hysterical, in cancan attire, flouncing their ruffled skirts. Singing. Tune: "I'm Late.")*

Oh dear, oh dear, we fear that we're too late.
So sorry that you had to wait, we know you had to wait.
And if we rush, there's still too much to do,
There just are not enough of us. And this is nothing new.

(A human-sized WHITE RABBIT from "Alice in Wonderland," with giant stopwatch, bounds across the stage.)

NURSE #1: I never called to change her diet!

NURSE #2: You seen her eat? She barely tries it--

NURSE #1: *(Hysterical.)* Her bed needs to be made!

NURSE #3: *(Under her breath.)*
How long since you got laid?

NURSE #2: I'm late in bringing her her pills.

NURSE #3: *(Under her breath.)*
I'm late in paying all my bills.

NURSE #1: I'm scared her vitals had to wait.
And I'm at least two hours late.

NURSE #2: Fudge it in the record.
She's not a fact collector.

JANE: *(Shouting. LOUD.)*
HAS ANYBODY SEEN MY LUNCH?!?!

(The NURSES freeze.)

BLACKOUT

SCENE 5. ON THE SCREEN:
"A WINTER WONDERLAND"

JANE: *(In her hospital bed, surrounded by pillows. White patch over one eye. Day.)* Medical science calls Myasthenia gravis "A SNOWFLAKE DISEASE." Because no two cases are alike. *(It starts to snow.)* So no one has a handle on mine. There is no "handle!" It's not a suitcase or a teapot.

(Manic, she emerges from her pillows in a shiny white tutu, toe shoes, sings. Tune: "I'm a Little Teapot.")

I'm a silly snowflake, thin and tall,
Got no handle, none at all.
This is so annoying. It's no fun!
Got no handle! FIND ME ONE!

(It's snowing harder.) Doctors just shove all kinds of pills at me. *(The MEDICINE BOTTLES rush in.)*

HUMAN-SIZED "MESTINON" PILL BOTTLE: Eat me! Eat me!

HUMAN-SIZED "BACTRIM" PILL BOTTLE: Eat me! Eat me!

HUMAN-SIZED "PREDNISONE" PILL BOTTLE: EAT ME! EAT ME--

JANE: It's Alice's Tea Party,

35

That's what's the matter.
And I am the Dormouse,
And I'm the Mad Hatter!

"Myasthenia" translates "Weak Muscles." They give me
Mestinon to help my double vision. Then I learn it
weakens my muscles. No wonder I'm going crazy.

*(Alice's MAD HATTER leaps across the stage in a white lab
coat. Disappears. From offstage we hear THE QUEEN OF
HEARTS: "OFF WITH THEIR HEADS!")*

JANE: *(Shivering under a foot of snow.)*
"A snowflake disease,"
my case like no other.
I'm cold. I'm scared.
I want my mother.…

BLACKOUT

SCENE 6. ON THE SCREEN: "BLIZZARD"

(JANE, white patch over one eye, shivers in her hospital wheelchair. Four feet of snow everywhere. Enter NURSES in heavy snow gear, fur hoods, short skis.)

NURSES: *(Singing. Tune: "Jingle Bells.")*
Through the rooms we go, bleary all the way,
What we wouldn't give for a one-horse open sleigh-hey!

JANE: I know you're doing your best.

NURSE #1: Two years Covid, did you guess:
No one's dealt with their PTS.

JANE: *(Singing. Tune: "White Christmas.")*
I'm praying for a sweet Christmas
Like all the ones from long ago,
Where I don't see double,
And chewing's no trouble,
And I'm not frozen in the snow.

I'm praying for a sweet-ass Christmas
Where what to do is always clear,
And where I'm not single,
Or maybe with Kris Kringle,
And I could have some wine or beer,

JANE: (Continued. Speaking.)
No one knows what's working.
The Prednisone?
The Mestinon?
The plasmapheresis?

It's a throw of the dice–
Did they test this on mice?

It's a crap shoot --
Except with my life!

BLACKOUT

SCENE 7. ON THE SCREEN:
"NIGHT"

(JANE asleep in her hospital bed. She is surrounded by VAMPIRE NURSES with Gothic black eye makeup, fangs, diamond tiaras, on roller skates.)

VAMPIRE NURSES:
Wake her up!
Shake her up!
Nab her!
Stab her!

GET HER BLOOD!

VAMPIRE NURSE #1: But sleep is so healing.
(Smiling.) We're just so unfeeling.

VAMPIRE NURSE #2: *(Salivating.)* Every three hours:
GET HER BLOOD!

VAMPIRE NURSES: *(Singing.)*
We will keep her busy,
Take her blood all through the night.
That could make her slightly dizzy,
We'll just take a tiny bite--

JANE: *(Deep in sleep. Rubbing her multi-punctured arm.)*
I'm a human piñata....
I'd like a frittata.

And maybe some cupcakes
and candy bars, too?!
(Gritted teeth.) Oh shit, I forgot:
There's no way I can chew–

(Wistful.) Then what about a chocolate cream?
PRAY GOD THAT THIS IS ALL A DREAM.

*(VAMPIRE NURSE #1 nudges Jane's arm. JANE wakes
with a start, falls out of bed. Cymbals Crash.)*

BLACKOUT

SCENE 8. ON THE SCREEN:
"THE MYASTHENIA MONSTER"

(A stand-off between JANE and THE MYASTHENIA MONSTER, a huge, long-haired, ash-colored beast, menacing and mean. JANE, on her walker, wearing a black patch, grabs her cane, threatens him.)

THE MYASTHENIA MONSTER: For all the good that will do you. There's not a medicine in sight to get me gone for good.

(He howls, victorious.)

And people have known about me for almost a hundred years!

JANE: *(Determined.)* I'm gonna knock you out of my ball park!

THE MYASTHENIA MONSTER: You just try!
I'll be with you your whole life.

JANE: *(Brandishing the cane.)* Get out! Get out--

THE MYASTHENIA MONSTER: *(Holds his ground.)*
If you're not careful, you could die.

JANE: If the hospital food doesn't kill me first.

(JANE performs a perfect karate punch at him,
accompanied by its classic war cry. He's impressed,
but she needs a breath. Then she hisses, barely audible:)

And I thought I was done with abusive relationships.

BLACKOUT

SCENE 9. ON THE SCREEN:
"AFTER TWELVE DAYS IN THE HOSPITAL"

JANE: *(Sitting up in bed, attached to an IV, orange patch on one eye. She removes the patch, squints, puts the patch back on. Sings. Tune: "The Hokey Pokey.")*

I got an IV here,
I got another there.
And it's eleven days
since I washed my hair.

The doctors come and go,
they hardly seem to care.
I thank my lucky stars
that I've got Medicare.

NURSE'S AIDE: *(Entering with JANE's lunch.)* Your puréed chicken.

JANE: Yummy-yum. The kitchen's chef should take a bow. This looks like a turd from a real live cow.

(A larger-than-life COW galumphs across the stage. She is followed by a line of DOCTORS and NURSES kicking like Rockettes.)

NURSE #1: Good news! Finally, you'll be going home--

DOCTORS: (*Singing. Tune: Be A Clown, Be A Clown, Be A Clown.*)
Let's hope you've hit your last plateau.
Though we don't know, we don't know, we don't know.

JANE: But I can't chew, I still see double!

NURSE #2: You'll still get infusions,
you'll still have confusions,

but sit outside, and under that pine—
You'll be fine, you'll be fine, you'll be fine.

DOCTOR #1: Just keep on taking all your meds.
(*Under his breath.*) It's just that we've run out of beds.

NURSE #1: They'll send you help. You'll be okay.
It's just you have to leave today!

BLACKOUT

END ACT ONE

ACT TWO

SCENE 1. ON THE SCREEN:
"JANE BACK HOME"

(A large artist's studio, pine trees outside. JANE, on her couch, wears a red patch and matching robe. Two CARE-GIVERS in kimonos in attendance. One holds a tray with a large teapot and cup. There's the gentle tinkling of a lute, until a marching band with three THERAPISTS enters. Maybe a tuba.)

PHYSICAL THERAPIST: *(Introducing himself.)* Your Physical Therapist.

OCCUPATIONAL THERAPIST: *(Introducing himself.)* Your Occupational Therapist.

SPEECH THERAPIST: *(Introducing herself.)* I'm going to help with your chewing and speech.

JANE: *(Under her breath.)* I think I would rather spend time at the beach.

(On the Screen: an inviting beach, seagulls flying.)

PHYSICAL THERAPIST: Let's see if you can walk....

47

SPEECH THERAPIST: Let's see how well you talk.

THERAPISTS: We will, we're going to make you well,
and so you know, this will be hell.

OCCUPATIONAL THERAPIST:
Can you get in the shower,
or in fact, do you cower?
We could put in a chair --
could you then wash your hair?

PHYSICAL THERAPIST: Let's do "The Chicken." Repeat
after me. (*Hands on his hips, elbows moving back and forth.
JANE does a very modified version. A CRAZED CHICKEN
flies through the air.*)
Now climb your fingers up the wall.
(*JANE tries.*) Bet you don't feel that at all.

JANE: (*In pain.*) I'm already going up the wall!
This was not a happy hour.
Could I have a whiskey sour?

THERAPISTS: (*Adamant. Together.*) NO!

JANE: I'll persevere, I'll stay on track.
I will not have this break my back.

(*She falls on her back, her legs straight up in the air.
Cymbals Crash.*)

BLACKOUT

SCENE 2. ON THE SCREEN:
"PHARMACEUTICALS"

(JANE, outside, sitting in a chair, under that pine, a cane by her side. Her dog on her lap. Green patch, green bathrobe. She tests her patch on and off, manic.)

JANE: Any issue, the doctors want to solve it with PHARMACEUTICALS! It's as if the companies were paying them. Crazy.

I tell my doctor the steroids are making me manic. He says, "You have a psychiatrist? There's a pill to keep you from being manic."

PHARMER: *(Enter a jolly FARMER, straw hat, holding a rake. Sings. Tune: "Old McDonald Had A Farm.")*
Old McPharma had a farm, ee-yi ee-yi oh.
And on that farm he had some drugs, ee-yi ee-yi oh.
With Retuxin here, and some Bactrim there,
Here a drug, there a drug, everywhere a drug, drug.

JANE: *(Singing. Juggling multi-colored patches.)*
With an eye patch here; and an eye patch there;
Here a patch, make it match.
Everywhere a patch, patch.

(We fade on her manic juggling.)

BLACKOUT

SCENE 3. ON THE SCREEN:
"A BODY AT WAR WITH ITSELF"

JANE: *(Inside, cross-legged on her couch, in an oval of light, attached to an IV. Purple patch, purple robe. CAREGIVERS in attendance.)*

(Singing.) My body at war with itself.
My country at war with itself.

CAREGIVERS: *(Back-up)* Doo-wah, Doo-wah! Doo-wah!

JANE: Democrats, against Republicans,
Republicans, against Republicans.
Democrats, against Democrats.
Populists, at war with autocrats.

CAREGIVERS: Doo-wah, Doo-wah! Doo-wah!

All around, countries at war to the death.
Our Earth is frying, with viruses doing the rest.

Everything threatens to do us all in.
My body's at war, and so I fit right in.

BLACKOUT

SCENE 4. ON THE SCREEN: "GAME SHOW"

(A game show. Bright lights read, "WAR OF THE DOCTORS." We see two closed doors. JANE, a contestant, watches, an orange patch over one eye, a blue patch off-center on her forehead.)

HOST: *(Hyper-energetic.)* And behind Door Number One– *(The door opens. GAME SHOW DOCTOR #1 leaps out.)* We have Doctor Number One!!

And from behind Door Number Two– *(The door opens. Out leaps GAME SHOW DOCTOR #2.)* We have Doctor Number Two!!

GAME SHOW DOCTOR #1: *(Roaring.)* Jane! Take Solaris!

GAME SHOW DOCTOR #2: *(Roaring.)* You should take Cellcept!

(The DOCTORS brandish swords, duel. They lunge and hit the other's heart at the end of every line.)

GAME SHOW DOCTOR #1: Solaris! *(Hit.)*

GAME SHOW DOCTOR #2: Could give her meningaris-- *(Hit.)*

GAME SHOW DOCTOR #1: Only a very small chance! *(Hit.)*

GAME SHOW DOCTOR #2: By the seat of her pants!

Give her the Cellcept. And quick! *(Hit.)*

GAME SHOW DOCTOR #1: But her poor little kidneys could get very sick. *(Hit.)*

JANE: *(Screaming.)* DOESN'T THE PATIENT GET A VOTE?

DOCTORS: *(LOUDER. At her.)* NO!!

GAME SHOW DOCTOR #1: Give her Vyvgard,
the drug is much newer! *(Hit.)*

GAME SHOW DOCTOR #2: Vyvgard, feh! Its trials are much fewer!
(He hits and wounds GAME SHOW DOCTOR #1, who falls on his back, legs straight up in the air, but before, who still manages to hit and wound GAME SHOW DOCTOR #2, who falls on his face. Cymbals Crash.)

JANE: *(Under a table, squeaking.)*
No more fighting!
NO MORE WAR!

BLACKOUT

SCENE 5. ON THE SCREEN:
"TANTRUM. TANTRUM!
After Five Months With MG"

(JANE, in her garden, wearing a flowered patch and matching robe, trying to cut some roses.)

CAREGIVER: *(Getting her into a chair.)*
You need to rest.
Or you won't get well.
And you'll get much worse;
and your life will be hell.

JANE: *(Flailing.)* REST!!?? When I was growing up it was a dirty word.

(Singing.) "Rest?!" It's a four-letter word,
Shit-dumbest word that I ever heard!

I'm used to making and baking
And moving and shaking,
Used to writing and dancing,
Rewriting, financing,

Used to theater enchantments,
To Botox enhancements,

JANE: *(Continuing.)*
Used to travel to Paris,
No shame and no hiding,
Used to falling and failing,
And rising and striding!

I'm a Type-A Personality,
I don't know what to do.
You said that I should "REST?!"
I DO NOT HAVE A CLUE!

BLACKOUT

SCENE 6. ON THE SCREEN:
"STEROIDS.
After Six Months"

(JANE, highly agitated, on a bench in her garden. Rose-colored patch, rose-colored dress. Next to her sits a handsome man wearing two large bottle-shaped placards: "STEROIDS" in front, "PREDNISONE" on the back.)

JANE: Thirty milligrams of Prednisone
<u>do</u> not have me "in the zone."
There are monkeys screaming in my head,
I've gained ten pounds.
....Well, at least I'm well-fed.

(Through gritted teeth.) Though it's still hard to chew!

PRINCE PREDNISONE:
I've made your toughest symptoms disappear.
You're moving hands and arms, my dear.
(In love. Gets on one knee.)
I'm hoping that you'll marry me. *(Offers a ring.)*
You'll gain forty pounds, you'll be a balloon,
and your cheeks and your face will be round as the moon.

JANE: *(Wary.)* I love the moon. I love pizza. That doesn't mean I want my face to look like one! And my memory's compromised--

PRINCE PREDNISONE: Like your immune system. Sorry. And there will be bone loss.

JANE: *(Almost the last straw.)* You're not exactly Santa Closs, "HO HO HO HO HO HO HO!"
(And I thought I was done with fucking snow.)

And I don't want to gain forty pounds, it took me forty years to get rid of the last ones! *(Manic glee.)* Maybe the doctors will take me off the Prednisone! No one knows if it's working or not. *(Now afraid.)* And maybe my symptoms will come back?

(Through gritted teeth.) At least they'll know what was helping.

PRINCE PREDNISONE:
(Singing. Tune: "You Are My Sunshine.")
You are my girl now, we'll have a whirl now,
You'll bring me blessings, and every day!
Too bad I'll ruin your mind and thinking,
Please don't take your steroids away!

JANE: *(Hissing.)* And I thought I was done with codependent, toxic relationships.

....At least he's not a liar.

BLACKOUT

SCENE 7. ON THE SCREEN:
"STILL NOT KNOWING.
After Seven Months"

JANE: (*On her couch, striped patch, matching striped robe, fetal position, clutching her dog.*)
It's a time of Not Knowing.
How bad is it snowing?

My going to Paris? The doctors don't even want me going into a 7-11. They've gunned down my immune system, so if someone had a cold, and I caught it, I'd have nothing to fight it with. Will I ever get to be with people again?.... And no one knows what drugs to give me.

(*Singing. Tune: "Let's Call The Whole Thing Off."*)
You say "Solahris," and I say "Solayris,"
All I want is a nice trip to Paris.
(*On the screen: Eiffel Tower, snow.*)
Polaris, Solayris,
Goodbye, trip to Paris.
Let's call the whole thing off!

But oh, if I took the drugs, then I could get a clot.
And oh, if I got a clot, then that could end the plot –

JANE: *(Continued.)* A big clot!
A small clot!
A blood clot!
I hope not!
Let's call the whole thing off!

(Speaking. Losing it.) I can't take it anymore....
I'm a snowflake.... I'm a seagull.

(Singing. Tune:"I'm a Little Teapot.")
I'm a silly seagull, tall and fat.
Why would I have thought of that?
Oh, I was an actress in the play,
But I don't know
WHO I AM TODAY....

(Speaking.) The doctors won't even let me have
a glass of wine.
"A glass of wine for when you dine?!"

"Not with your meds!"
say the fucking genius heads.

AND I DON'T EVEN DRINK!

(Out of an innocent-looking bag come three bottles of wine. JANE drinks them, is drunk, cuckoo, throws the empty bottles in the air. They land with a crash on the floor. She's lost it.)

I'm a snowflake.... I'm melting....
Will I ever get better, will I walk, will I see?
Will this go on forever? This just isn't me.

*(She gives up, flat on her back. Her GRAMMA
ESTHER flies in, hovers overhead. In shtetl clothes.)*

GRAMMA: *(Russian accent.)* Janela?

JANE: *(Trying to sit up.)* Gramma, is that you?

GRAMMA: Yes, Bubbela. You're going to be fine. I
want you to know how much I love you.

JANE: *(Starts to cry.)* I love you too, Gramma.
I wish you weren't dead.

GRAMMA: *(Smiling.)* But you can hear me
in your head.

Oooh, I wish I could give you a bagel. Some cream
cheese. Some nova. Tomato. You need to keep up your
strength.

It doesn't matter I'm really not real,
Just take in my love, it really could heal.
It really could heal.

JANE: *(Crying.)* I love you so much, Gramma--

GRAMMA: I know, sweetheart. You know I love you, too --

(And GRAMMA is gone.)

JANE: *(New color in her cheeks. Looks into the sky, shakes her fist.)* I'm gonna be fine. So what if the doctors don't know what's working. They're only human. Nobody's perfect...

(An epiphany. She smiles.)

Only snowflakes are perfect.

BLACKOUT

EPILOGUE

ON THE SCREEN:
"SEVEN MONTHS IN"

JANE: (*In fuchsia-colored patch and matching sundress, in her garden, her dog in her lap. CAREGIVERS at hand. JANE takes off her patch, tests her vision, leaves it off. Sings. Tune: "Home, Home on the Range."*)

I'm back in my home, where the caregivers roam,
And my dog and the therapists play,
Where my walk's getting better,
And my dog – I can pet her,
And the doctors don't get in the way.

CAREGIVER #1: In another six months, I hope they'll have balanced your meds.

JANE: I can take off the patches once in a while.
I still cannot chew, but at least I can smile.

CAREGIVER #2: (*Compassionate.*) Seems like the terrible War between Your Immune System and Your Body -- may be winding down--

JANE: Peace! Please! Between My Body and Me!
And let me forgive it for getting MG.

(DOVE with olive branch appears in the sky.)

JANE: *(Singing. Tune: "My Country 'Tis of Thee.")*
My country of MG, sweet land of misery,
To thee I sing.
Land of the doctors' pride, land where the patients cried,
From each and every weary side,
LET FREEDOM RING!

(On the screen and on stage: a magical landscape. Lush trees and flowers. DOCTORS and NURSES enter, many wearing colored patches. JANE squints, puts her patch back on.)

The dreadful symptoms could return -- Or not.
It's the end of the play. But not of the plot.

NURSE #1: She's a comedy writer,
some people don't get her.

DOCTOR #1: But Jane, you're a fighter,
I bet you'll get better!

JANE: I'll be dancing in no time.
(She dons a top hat, takes her IV pole as her partner.)

GRAMMA: *(In the sky, in shtetl clothing, looking younger than before.)*
You'll shine. You'll be fine, I'm not wrong.
Janela, eat. You need to be strong.

(A rain of diamond-studded bagels falls from the sky.)

JANE: Am I dreaming?

DOCTOR #2: *(Singing.)* "All your dreams can come true..."

(BLUEBIRDS appear in the sky.)

JANE: But I'm programmed to be driven.

(Fancy, shiny cars drive across the stage.)

But I'll learn how to rest.
I'll master the lesson. I WILL PASS THE TEST.

(The rest of the cast appears on stage: WHITE RABBIT, MAD HATTER, CLOWN, HUMAN-SIZED TURKEY, SHERLOCK HOLMES DOCTORS, GIRAFFE, COW, etc.)

(Singing. Tune: "Somewhere.") There's a life for me,
For living with MG,
Peace for all, for the dove and cow....
SOMEHOW--

WHOLE CAST: *(Singing, dancing, jubilant.)*
There's a life for us,
With jokes and rhymes for us,

NURSES: *(Singing, overlapping, as other cast members reprise their signature melodies, all overlapping in perfect harmony.)* Oh dear, oh dear, we don't want to be late. It's an important date. We'd hate for you to wait.

JANE: *(Overlapping. Tune: "I Feel Pretty.")*
I feel hopeful, and I'm happy,
And it's sappy how happy I feel –

DOCTORS: *(Overlapping. Happy. Tune: "Be a Clown.")*
We don't know, we don't know, we don't know.

GRAMMA: *(Overlapping.)* We'll all dine. We'll be fine.

RAVEN: *(Overlapping.)* Evermore. Evermore.

WHOLE CAST: *(Tune: "Somewhere.")*
Peace for all, and health! And NOW!
SOMEHOW....

(JANE rips off her eye patch. DOCTORS and NURSES rip off theirs, throw the multi-colored patches into the air. The sky is lit not only with the sparkling bagels, but also with The Dance of the Patches. The curtain falls.)

THE END

Part II. POEMS, PRAYERS AND HEALING
The Next Seven Months,
April, 2021 – October, 2022

MG

I know people die of it.
I know I make light of it.

It's still good to do it.
The trick's to get through it.

WATER SKIING INTO THE NEW YEAR

"The goal with Myasthenia is always
to get the patient back to water skiing."
– Dr. Stanley T. Carmichael, Chair, Department of
Neurology, David Geffen School of Medicine, UCLA

Water skiing! Again? Wind in my face?!
Aliveness?! This Myasthenia gravis won't
keep me from swimming, goddammit, even
with a wildly compromised immune system!

I will live wildly again! No more
living on eggshells!
(Drugs, maybe.)

A pox on the warnings, horror stories,
graveness of the disease!
(They had to add the "Gravis?")

As the doctor said, NO MORE EGG SHELLS!
Here's to egg salads at picnics;
omelets in France; ocean spray; speed.
Adventure! Daring! Muscle strength, balance,
ALIVENESS!

Thank you, doctor.

COYOTE

This MG,
this coyote trickster,
makes you think that all is well –
then attacks:

One day I see the world
the way I did before MG,
next day I see double,
blurry, triple.

Sleight of the eye.

MY HOSPITAL VISITORS

They came. Eight of them. Heroes. And in the time of Covid. I will always be grateful.

My actress friend, who they wouldn't let into the hospital because she didn't have her driver's license. So her husband brought up the soup and sat with me, and my friend cried outside on the curb. An actress reluctant to let anyone see her license with her real age on it.

My Neighborhood Organizer came. Got a problem? Call her – for a dog run over, or a child who wants to learn to sing. She came bearing gifts: an orchid plant, a book of poems, massage cream, chocolates. And her brother came, taller than all my doctors.

My director friend came, could barely fit in the hospital chair, the hospital too small for all the love he carried. And my brave, loyal assistant came, carrying a soup she knew I'd like and wouldn't have to chew.

My retired press agent friend brought soft sushi and what seemed to me to be a very rare orchid plant, its ruffled petals fuchsia, white, and burgundy. Colorful, multi-layered, like our friendship.

My spiritual guru brought cotton pants which I'd told her I needed – in shocking pink, no less. She also brought comfort and love. The world's best medicines.

What makes a person love you enough to drive an hour to see you, and to a hospital no less, where Covid is still a danger to doctors, nurses and guests alike?

Maybe it's enough just to acknowledge the gift, marvel, and be grateful.

SEEING WITH NEW EYES

They can't give me new glasses with fancy prisms to help me not see double. Because my shape-changing disease can switch my muscles on and off. And the glasses would work one day, but not another.

When I returned home from the hospital, I was shocked to see that three neighbors, with whom I had had maybe one meal over eighteen years, learning I would be home from the hospital

WASHED MY SHEETS?!
PUT CLEAN ONES ON MY BED?!
CLEANED OUT MY FRIDGE?!
VACUUMED MY CARPETS?!
THEY CLEANED MY HOUSE??!!

Had I ever seen they even liked me?
Had I seen I had neighbors who cared?
How much I didn't see!

Seeing the world with new eyes.
Not bad.

GASLIT

Myasthenia gravis. It's not like strep
or pneumonia, where you take
an antibiotic and you're better.

One MG doctor told me how well his patients
were doing on Retoxin, a non-steroidal
immune suppressant. Then I learn
Mass General is warning doctors
not to give it to immune-suppressed patients
because if they got Covid they would likely die.

Another doctor tells me: "You need Naltrexone."
Another says: "It's counter-indicated
for Myasthenia gravis."

Another doctor: "IVIGs are good for you."
Another, "We'll want to get you off of them."
All honorable men. Different opinions –

"That's what makes horse races,"
my father would say.

But away from the track
they could make a person crazy.

ARISTOTLE ONASSIS' MYASTHENIA

Did he not want to see
he would always love
the world's most famous opera singer,
a working girl? And he a prince,
ship magnate, multi-millionaire.

No use his being named after
the famous Greek philosopher,
both of them in love with logic,
music, metaphysics.
Still, how could he ever understand
the logic of his eyelids falling closed?

Did he not want to see that he was
vulnerable? That he had MG? That all his
millions couldn't fix him, or that
his drooping lids would finally need
to be sewn up to their very brows?

Was it his very own personal
Betsy Ross that stitched them up,
a hidden message from America
to marry our former First Lady,

the iconic Jackie Kennedy?
(And did he ever truly see <u>her</u>?)

How could he have loved the opera singer
for so long and left her, and he,
like his ancient namesake, a lover
of music and metaphysics? Surely some of her
high notes had revamped his very cells.

But he left Callas for Jackie
(odd, the seduction of shiny things)

and he left Jackie
to go back to
the music.

SURPRISE!

It's not like they can tell you
On the twenty-third day,
you will get a very high fever
and you will die.

It's more like
On the twenty-third day?
We haven't a clue.
Maybe you'll barely walk or see.
It'll be a surprise.

Not like when we were kids
and didn't know what
we'd be getting for Christmas.
A surprise.
Probably a nice one.

Surprises.
Maybe my house burns down.
Or maybe I meet my soul mate.

Gotta be ready.

ORGASMS

I may have weak eye muscles,
weak hand muscles, weak leg muscles,
but glory be to God, my pelvic muscles
that froze with early childhood molestation --
are now sooooo relaxed!

So now – explosions! Floods!
And the sweet smell of cucumber juice
and fragrant rose water.

Here I am angry about my MG,
feeling lost, afraid – and my body
insists there are, still, deep, unfathomable,
before unimaginable pleasures
that I thought were myth.

There have to be some perks to this insanity.

ME, CLOWN

This circus has too many rings! Too many
pills to juggle! Too many doctors,
like clowns somersaulting,
too many nurses on invisible high wires
shooting brightly colored needles at me.

I can't juggle as well as I used to --
thirty years ago I was the Ringmaster Clown
with Circus Flora, my face painted
clown white, a black line down
the left side of my face, so carefully,
cleverly, reverently drawn
by the old Yugoslav master.

AND HOWEVER DID I MAKE SO MANY
CHILDREN SCREAM WITH LAUGHTER?

Was it the makeup? Or the pink, embroidered,
satiny slippers with pointy toes that no prince
would ever try on my feet again?
Or did my costume, deep purple and bejeweled,
have me spinning, making faces, dancing, almost

falling? I couldn't stop them laughing, me cawing,
arms swooping, juggling the air, prat-falling,
then twirling, then smiling, then bowing.

These days I juggle IVs and steroids,
one doctor's opinions with another's,
one night's sweats with the next day's chills.

Could I imagine my eyes
circling comical full circles –
and not seeing blurry
or scary? Not seeing double?!

These days I juggle wearing a patch,
then not a patch, then on, then off,
and on and off again.
I juggle medicine schedules, me and my dog
jumping through hoops.

Could I dream of balancing on an index finger,
or my dog upside down on one paw
on a bright red rubber ball?

How do I keep me and the children
screaming with laughter?
Because laugh we must.

And the show must go on.

PIRATE JANE

I wear a patch,
a one-eyed pirate

wanting
if not willing

to steal
or kill

for my old
eyes.

"A SNOWFLAKE DISEASE"

Myasthenia gravis.
"A snowflake disease."
No two cases alike.

More like a snow storm.
No, an avalanche.

Focus
on making
The Perfect
Snow
Angel.

TO LIZA WITH NPH, FROM ME WITH MG

"This crazy horse disease
just runs away with me,"
you said about your NPH, your
Normal Pressure Hydrocephalus.

Me, I got a crazy horse myself –
comes with my Myasthenia.
Some nerve! Your nerves and mine --
attacked and down!
(Well, not performing up to snuff.)

You have "a gait disease,"
but the gaits of our wayward horses
are not elegant. Or helpful.
THEY'RE WILD
AND OUT OF CONTROL!

My crazy horse immune system
is hyperactive, ADHD (too many dead initials
for stuff that's so alive!), attacking what it should
protect (also a sad and human trait).

Would our crazy horses trotted us
to the Crazy Horse Café in 1920's Paris

and we'd sit at a table, smell the macaroons,
have double espressos and almond croissants,
and thrill to F. Scott Fitzgerald, James Joyce
and Ernest Hemmingway at tables nearby.
(Surely, writers are the best crazy horses --
witness this poem full of arcane abbreviations.)

On one of the café's shelves – please! –
is there a book to teach us how to
put bits in the mouths of our rude, unruly beasts
that wobble our walking, and paralyze our nerves,
so that we tame them, and then you and I
could ride together
into some lush and happy landscape?!

And maybe we two become crazy horses ourselves,
and horse around, braying and neighing
and joking and smoking
and laughing and running around
just having a good time?!

And then those other crazy horses just
go to sleep, with dreams so powerful
and deep, those horses have no need of us,
just of their own, rich, fast-riding,
healing sleep.

SUDDENLY!

Suddenly, I'm Rubenesque. Like the women
in paintings by Rubens, 16th century genius.
Enormous. Massive. Giant. Whopping.

I used to be
skinny. An
El Greco.
A Giacom-
metti.

Now I look like I'm going to give birth to
twin hedgehogs. Not that I've ever seen a hedgehog.
My stomach hard as footballs. Steroids will do that.

But it's
2023,
and
what's
"in"
is
thin.

Big bellies are out. Ha ha ha ha ha. I look like one of
those strapping female statues in bronze in the

outdoor garden of the Museum of Modern Art
in New York where I grew up. Heft. Tires. Bulk.

Nothing
like
my old
lithe
dancer's
body,
torso
stream-
lined,
one
straight
line
from
thigh
to
waist,
a young
thin tree
growing
upwards.

MAYBE MY LESSON IS DARING TO BE AN AMAZON
QUEEN, READY AND ABLE TO FIGHT MY DISEASE.
MIGHTY. INDOMITABLE. UNYIELDING.
VICTORIOUS.

RANTS ONE OF MY NERVES

"Oh, Muscle! Can you hear me?
Oh, MUSCLE! I have a message for you!
(This is so frustrating!!)
Jaw muscle, get chewing!
Jane loves to chew, to eat, to live.
Get it together! Get a life!

"I'M SCREAMING AT THE TOP OF MY LUNGS!
WHY CAN'T YOU HEAR ME?
Is there anything more important than
Communication? Yes, health!
Help!"

The muscle cannot hear the nerve yelling
as if to reach the very last seats in a Greek
amphitheater (*Myasthenia* from the Greek).

The nerve and I are screaming,
the way I sense, outside in the world,
people are screaming --
Words. Warnings. Opinions.

And too often, it seems,
nobody is listening.

CYCLOPS JANE

I use one eye.
I got a patch on the other.
Darkness.

It worked okay for
Polephemus
until Odysseus
did the Cyclops in.

Never mess with
journeymen
with a purpose.

HEY! YOU! MY ANTIBODIES!

What's going on, guys? You're attacking
what you should hold holy.
Could you all just calm down?

What's up with you?! Brawling? Dancing?
Singing? You fighting, drunk? Bacchanalian revels
do often turn deadly.

All those scientists, any of them
ever gone in there, got a good look?

Hey, you! My antibodies! How can I
help you do your proper work?
Maybe put you in some clean, crisp
straightjackets, calm you down,
feed you happy food, soup and chocolate,
bread and butter,
so you have no need
of my once happy, healthy body.
And all of us will be at peace.

ANIMAL SPIRIT

I will hatch a new life,
and for now not resist
being a scruffy duck
wobbly on matchstick legs,
eyes not focused,
seeing double, triple.
Vision blurry.

Surely I will know that
soon, someday,
I will find wings.
And fly.

"IT'S MANAGEABLE"

That's what my first doctor told me.
"MG. It's manageable."

When I was an actress, I had a manager.
She managed to do nothing.

My doctor's words I suppose
were meant to be calming,
but only left me confused.

Would it be like being with the manager
who did nothing? It was I who
got me *Rocky* movies, TV series,
the Lincoln Center gigs.

Somehow, my manger managed
to eat, and live in a nice house.
And so did I.
So not all bad.

"Manageable."

TOTAL EXHAUSTION

MG Fatigue, like a lazy wolf,
suddenly sleeps on top of me
its fur coat stultifying, suffocating.

Have to learn to sleep with it,
nap with it, surrender.

This wolf, not in sheep's clothing,
has brutally pulled me to the ground.
But I must fight.
I am Little Red Riding Hood
and my grandmother is dead.

He doesn't even pretend to be her,
drapes over me as if he would melt,
like a hot blanket, like a Dali clock.

And I haven't the slightest clue,
at all, about what time it is.

COMPLAINING

It's allowed.
But not to get carried away.
So many people have it worse –

Like my New York painter friend
scared of going blind
from macular degeneration.
I have the poster from her show in Paris
in my bedroom: A nude,
a naked woman in a chair –
graceful, sensual, relaxed.

Or like my painter friend
in Seattle, who had a stroke
and cannot hold a brush.
I have a painting of hers,
also in my bedroom:
a six-by-six foot, almost window
of a painting, of trees after rain,
dark trunks and splotchy leaves.

Me, I have my hands again,
and enough vision to write –

not all the time, not always easily,
but eventually.
If I rest.

I love my painter friends,
I love their paintings. I imagine the trees,
smell their rain. I am the nude.
We are all naked.

Part III. POEMS, RANTS AND HOPE
The Next Seven Months,
November, 2022 – May, 2023

SQUIRREL

MG's so slowed me down that this morning,
before rare, instead of always doing "stuff –"
washing dishes, reading emails,
putting clothes away or writing a poem,
I look out my glass doors,

and at the far corner of my deck
under its red umbrella,
I see a squirrel,
sitting on its hind legs!

It doesn't matter that my dog, inside,
barks at him to go away,
the squirrel doesn't budge.
And he keeps on coming back.

I search the meaning of the Squirrel Totem:
"New Balance. New Life. Perseverance. Productivity."
Yes, witness this book.
I love this squirrel.

And it squeaks! Maybe it's a song.
I have to pay attention,
it's probably a good one.

EXPERIMENTAL

The doctor confesses
I'm "an experiment."
Ha ha ha ha ha ha ha!

He and I laugh together:
"I'm an experiment."
"You're an experiment."

"I'm an experiment."
"You're an experiment."

It's not funny.

ON MUSIC

I must orchestrate
a new life for myself.

Where's the bassoon?

Must create a schedule based on
when to take what pills with meals,
what pills without.
No soft pedal on the piano.

Must wear clothes that protect me
from sun (thanks to my new drug,
a wily, flamingo-pink and
powder-blue rock 'n' roll capsule).

Must boycott parties, indoor restaurants,
theaters, stores, my immune system
compromised. Must learn to live fully
without travel or meeting new people,
for duets and trios
(piano, clarinet, cello).

Bring in the violins! But how to find
Romance, since doctors insist

I barely leave the house?!

(Would I, could I, hear a flute!
I remember playing one in school
when I was healthy, strong.)

I need a bass line, new grounding.
And could I have a xylophone for humor?

Still, slowed down, I finally get to see
the birds outside my window, see their
beating wings, accomplished metronomes.
Did I ever, really, hear their music?

Still, no bassoon.

"If music be the food of love"
then let me stuff my face with it,
my mouth, my ears with it! More Mozart!
Beethoven! Schubert, Schumann!
Music in the nostrils, Haydn smelling like
roast pigeon. Eat more Jellyroll Morton,
more Brahms, more Gershwin
than a hundred pigs in a hungry trough!
Folk songs for my liver,

show tunes for my heart.
Sacred hymns as yet unknown.

I think of my old friend, Boris Brott,
and all the concerts he conducted.
At eighty-two, that Canadian had more energy
than one hundred squirrels running for their lives.
And then he got hit by a car. Crossing the street
in front of his house. A hit and run.
Dead six hours later, his wife screaming
in the ambulance all the way to the hospital.
Dead just like that. Music or no music.

Must learn to be
my own first-class conductor.
Orchestrate. Compose. Bow.
Make more music
than I already know.

ONLY IN LA

When I first met my present
Primary Caregiver, she admitted
she knew nothing about MG.
Few do. She's learning.

Our last appointment, hearing of
my MG doctors' silences and opposite opinions,
perhaps she feels my frustration, confusion
and despair; and my brilliant LA doctor,
my smart, kind and caring LA doctor,
has finally only one suggestion:
she gives me the number of her
ASTROLOGER!

"Maybe," she says, "she can tell us
when this difficult period will end."

Mock LA as you will, or me, or her,
I call the astrologer. She tells me
I'll have to wait for a reading,
her house burned down a year ago
in the Marshall Fire, she's moving,
she's not centered, can I wait?

I mention my own house burned down in 2000
and that I wrote an article about it
for *The Los Angeles Times.* The next day
she texts me that she's read it,
that she feels so much better, feels
someone understands. And I feel better.

Then she shows it to her neighbors
who'd also lost their homes. They feel better.
And now I'm really feeling better.

Maybe calling the astrologer
wasn't such a dumb idea, after all.

MY EYES

Once "my best feature."
But wandering today,
not at all aligned.
Once so expressive,
their old color even
rare, powerful,
grey/green/blue,
bright but not blinding
(windows to the soul).

Maybe like a pianist's fingers
that suddenly won't work,
or an athlete's legs
that won't obey.

Did I overinvest
in my so-called strength?
Was it Vanity? Hubris?

Never mind.
At least I can see.

I AM HUNGRY FOR ADVENTURE!

For newness! But I can't leave
my little neighborhood and visit
restaurants, stores, museums, or airports,
my hazmat suit uncomfortable.

Still, walking the dog this morning,
I stop to look at an oak at the side of the road,
there since I moved here nineteen years ago.
Did I ever really see it? *Really* see it?
The lace of the leaves, their green of shiny hope,
deep as ocean unexplored? These phoenix oaks!
Sole survivors of our fires.

New! I see it new! The mirroring leaves,
the patterning branches, the covering blanket.

I decide to make friends with the oak.
A new friend.
New adventure.

SEE ME! SEE ME!

I wanted to be a star
for my mother.
Her dream, my body.

I was a good little girl,
I starred on Broadway, even had
a photo of myself in *Harper's Bazaar*,
me in a fancy dress
making a pseudo-glamorous face.

Actresses have so many photos
taken of themselves!
Who doesn't want to be seen?!
Actresses *really* want to be seen.

And I've never had more photos
taken of me than since I got MG –
you get sick, they take a lot of photos,
you don't even have to be a star!

Doctors scared I'm having mini-strokes?
Take a picture of my brain!
(So intriguing.)

Doctors want to check for cancer --

Photograph my uterus!
(Exquisite intimacy.)

And photograph those intestines!
They wear no makeup,
do not pose! What a relief.
And that pituitary gland –
so elegant, that little general.

And my thymus!
Having a jolly breakdown I'll bet.
And the crazy irony is: if diseased,
they'd take it out, and I'd have
no more symptoms! Ha ha ha ha ha.
But mine is just fine.

So many photos!
Surely extreme measures
just to be seen.

Mommy, Mommy,
I don't want to be a movie star,
I just want to be loved.

I BUY A NEW COAT

Chic as shit. From a catalog.
(Of course. I don't go out.)
Flawless fit. Fit for Paris.
If I ever go there again.

Dark loden green.
Skirt mid-calf, with a pleat in the back
that opens and swings,
the shoulders elegantly capped.

And then there's the lining:
BRIGHT YELLOW!
BRIGHTEST YELLOW!
Silky! Shiny! The Happy Color!
OUTRAGEOUS!
Open that coat! Swish that skirt!
FLAP AND FLAUNT THAT NEON LINING!

Surely the coat will help me
fashion My New Identity --

as in "Chic and Hilarious?"
"Sassy, snazzy, and still serious?!"

The coat's silliness makes me smile,
makes me <u>happy</u>.
Add <u>that</u> to my New Identity!
Clearly more fun than my older, scholarly,
too serious, Compulsive Worker Self.

Court jesters always had the brightest,
most colorful, most original wardrobes.
They made people laugh.
And they were also wise.

TIA MIA

They forgot to tell me
my infusions of immunoglobulin
thicken the blood. They forgot to tell me,
"Drink lots of water because
no one wants thick blood,
the blood could have trouble
getting to your brain."

And now they're afraid I've had a "ministroke."
A TIA. Because I've seen black spots at night.
A Transient Ischemic Attack. Sounds like
a country near Latvia or Czechoslovakia.

Actually, it sounds like a place
where you can't speak right
or think right.
And nobody told me.

For thirty years, children in Topanga
call me "Auntie Jane."
In Spanish, "TIA JUANA."
Not the Mexican city.
"Auntie Jane."

I get an MRI, an MRA.
For both my head and my neck,

both with contrast.
AND I AIN'T GOT NO TIA'S!

Maybe because I play with the children.
Maybe because they see me and call out,
"Auntie Jane! Auntie Jane!" Maybe because
I play with them, with my dog.
With words. Don't shoot me:
There's Auntie Inflammatories, Auntie Bodies,
Auntie Terrorists. Auntie Trust laws.
Maybe because I play.

People say, what with Covid, and the new flu,
and a new respiratory disease,
I should stay away from children.

But I want to play with the children!
I want to play as children play.
What could be more healing.

CELLCEPT AND THE SUN

Before I swallow the pill
the package warns me
AVOID THE SUN
OR YOU'LL GET
CANCER.

So no dancing in the sun,
or with the sun in Maypole rays of light.
I am robbed of my primal Salute to The Sun,
my body celebrating what gives our planet
LIFE.

They told us Sun could kill the Corona virus!
That star's our friend. Even doctors tell you,
"To feel better, sit in the sun."
Myasthenia gravis may be my foe,
but, surely, not the Sun.

My friend Harry, with a double lung transplant,
also takes Cellcept, so that his immune system
won't attack the implants. Am I that far gone?

Apparently. And he gets cancer cells
regularly burned off his face.

What kind of sadistic drug is this
that keeps us from the source of
LIFE? Really guys, can't you
come up with something better?
Eastern, even Western thinkers, tell us God
is Light, and you want to keep me from it?

It's "an immune *suppressant?*" You'd think
that a person who's sick would need
all the immune *support* she could get.
So is this a medicine or a sick joke?

———

I try the pill for ten whole weeks.
Then I get chills, cold sweats.
I think the pill's the culprit.
I quit. My doctors have no opinions.
I am, after all, an experiment.

I'm told to avoid the sun
for three more months.
But then I can dance with the sun.
With the sun!

TWENTY-SEVEN REASONS TO BE GRATEFUL

I'm grateful that I can finally walk without wobbling. And that I can talk. And can be understood. I'm grateful that I can laugh and make other people laugh. I'm grateful that I sometimes feel hopeless, and that I emerge, like a whale from the depths, into the light.

I'm grateful I have mountains and trees close to my house and that I sometimes remember they have lessons for me. I'm grateful there's a café around the corner so that in the morning I can go sit on the patio before too many people get there who may be sick. So that I'm around people and have human contact, so my body can produce some serotonin, which will support my immune system. I'm grateful that I can feel grateful.

I'm grateful I can write (this book). I'm grateful I love food and that I can chew again. I'm grateful I can once again spread my fingers like a starfish. I'm grateful I can lift my arms up over my head again, as if celebrating a victory. Which I am.

I'm grateful that if I bruise myself and that it's even black-and-blue, that I sometimes remember remedies that can heal it, and I use them. I'm grateful for flowers, and deer, and coyotes, and people who are kind, generous and loving. I'm grateful for my grandmothers.

I'm grateful when I don't see double. I'm grateful when I feel I understand one of my doctors. I'm grateful that my dog sleeps on my bed, so in the morning I can reach out and touch another living being that loves me - maybe not a human, but this helps me feel I'm not alone.

I'm grateful that my dog is a good caretaker. He even refuses to go out if I seem too sick to take him out. I'm grateful that he is always sympathetic when I'm feeling sad or glad or crazy angry. I'm grateful that my dog is healthy, and doesn't have MG.

RHYMES

When we brought down the dose of
my immunoglobulin infusions,
my eyes got worse. We upped the dose.
Eyes still bad. For no apparent
rhyme or reason.

I want rhyme! I want reason! But this MG –
my eyes see double and blurry one day,
and the next, they work just fine
AND FOR NO APPARENT RHYME
OR REASON!

The doctors, not rhyming, haven't a clue –
Is it the dosage or the disease
that makes my eyes
better one day, worse the next?

Science, full of reason,
proves that rhyming

balances the right hemispheres
of our brains.

Rhyme. Mime.
Time. Chime.
Lime. Prime.
Ginny Keim
(high school classmate).

MG must have reasons of its own. Me, I got
rhymes, exactly one hundred seventy-seven
in this book alone. For no reason.

Except they make me happy.

WHO ME, ANGRY?

How to swallow the rage?
Today's nurse stabs me
four times
before getting the needle in.

Go ahead, I hear you saying,
Let it go. Water off a duck's back.
Except I'm not any kind of
feathery, flurrying, water-floating
goddamned duck.

Last week three doctors thought
I'd been having mini-strokes
from my infusions
because my left eye, twice,
saw black. Just black. Scary.
I saw red.

Go ahead, I hear you saying,
Hey, take it in stride. Except my stride,
MG compromised, ain't what it used to be.

This week, my primary's phlebotomist,

who before had never missed a vein,
had to try twice to get a needle in –
to get some blood, to analyze
WHAT WE PROBABLY WILL NOT KNOW
IS GOING ON.

And now my arm, where he missed the vein,
is black-and-blue.
But I see red.

Go ahead, I hear you saying,
ACCEPTANCE is the key!
SURRENDER!

Fuck you.

And that anger, where does it belong?
Under a rug? Trust me,
whatever belongs under that rug
doesn't fit in anybody's pocket.

I'd asked for a faster MRI,
so if I'd had those mini strokes,
we'd know in less than seven days
if I were having them.
My doctor ordered one, but forgot to ask

for one of head and <u>neck</u>.
So now I have to wait two weeks
for the second MRI,
and I have trouble sleeping,
thinking I'm having mini-strokes.
I worry.

Why can't I be more like
Alfred E. Newman, poster boy for
MAD Magazine, endlessly smiling, saying,
"WHAT, ME WORRY?"

I try to smile,
and make "a happy face,"
AND TRY NOT TO
PUNCH SOMEONE OUT.

I did it, I punched no one out!!
But there's no prize. Just more blood tests
and infusions…And I'm walking around
LOOSE?
Is it safe for anyone?
Is it safe for <u>me</u>?

At least I'm not driving.

The last three needle stabs
left a deep black and blue cloud shape

on my arm. A cloud shaped like –
a nurse about to stab me with a needle?

Or is it a message:
"Soon it will rain.
Get out your umbrella."

I have a great raincoat.
Presumably it covers everything.

MG FATIGUE

Must take naps.
NAPS, spelled backwards, "SPAN."
As in I must see the span of my life,
allow perspective. I've had it pretty good.

But these sudden hits of fatigue are hard
because I want to edit this book
AND I'M EXHAUSTED.
Too often, I have to a take a NAP.

NAP backwards is PAN, which is
no help at all unless I'm cooking up
something delicious, always a possible cure –
Pleasure! When mixed with serotonin
THEY STRENGTHEN THE IMMUNE SYSTEM!

So how about some eggs and cheese? In butter.
Mushrooms and zucchini? More butter!
(No accident that serotonin's
manufactured in the gut.)

Or maybe I could just whip myself up

a plain, old-fashioned, chocolate
chocolate hot fudge brownie!?

Or I could imagine the camera PANS
the landscape out my window,
the green mountains and the stalwart trees.

Am exhausted, yes,
but spanning and panning –
it's not so bad.

ME, ONE-EYED BANDIT

Early morning at the café.
Me in a colored patch.
And matching dress. Word Pirate,
my books flying off the shelves,
my dog's ears like airplane wings.
Mainly my *Dog Poems* flying off the shelves.

Does it matter I see double
unless I wear a patch,
I can still see!?

And if I close my eyes, might I understand
the multiples of the universe,
way beyond my seeing double --
to see my dog here, and in our next lives,
to see my sister here, and in past lives together?
To see maybe a million more of everything –
cafés to come, cafés past; dogs to come, canines past;
books, buildings, millions, over millions of years.
Trillions of stars over infinite galaxies.

And I'm only seeing double.

TUTORIAL

No lazy brain me!
I'm learning new skills:
Like how to remember
To take all my pills;

To take doctors' opinions
With good grains of salt;
To learn to accept this
(Not what I was taught);

To learn to be grateful,
In even tough times;
To accept my disease;
And persist with my rhymes.

THE NURSE BRIGADE

Every two weeks, a nurse comes to my house.
It's a seven-hour infusion. Drip. Drip. Plop. Plop.
Plasma from two hundred-forty strangers.
Who are they? An astronaut? An opera singer?
A sociopath or serial killer? Are they all
having a party? It'd be a big one.
That's a lot of strangers swimming,
running, coursing through my veins.

I've had over two dozen nurses
these last fifteen months. When they enter,
do they throw off invisible capes
heavy with their last patient's illnesses,
their last patient's sadnesses? Do they bring
their own dreams? Do their disappointments
fly around my living room?
Do they stick to the walls?
Do they bring their parents' problems,
maybe their ancestors' DNA
with its special gifts and challenges?
Should I be burning sage after they leave.

Before they come, I clean up, want to make
a good impression. I want them to like me.
After all, they'll hold my life blood in their
needle-plunging fingers.
Sometimes I feel that if I don't make

people like me, they could kill me.
I have to remind myself:
I do not have to entertain them.
This isn't Broadway.
This is my life.

At the least, surely, I have to be polite,
talk, answer questions. Most of them
are hungry. I can hear them, silent:
Feed me. Feed me with answers.
Tell me about your life, your acting.
Exhausting.

Not all the nurses have been stellar.
One couldn't get a needle into a vein
until the fourth try, my arm black and blue
for weeks. Another bragged he was into
real estate, did I want to sell my house?!

A lot of them tell me
of their own
autoimmune diseases –
which somehow doesn't cheer me up.

And did I really want to hear one nurse
telling me about the man she married,

who had just become a woman,
and the nurse had never been comfortable
with women?!

I understand. We all so need to tell our stories.
Still, it's a lot of information.

They're from all over: the US, Russia, China,
Mexico, the Philippines. They invade my house
with their countries' histories, their countries' heroes,
their relief at being in America,
their wanting to be "100% American,"
and their pain at not fitting in. I feel it all.

Have I no empathy?
Too much.
And no Boundaries! I take in their pain,
and they're supposed to be taking care of me.

One nurse asks me, "How many languages do you speak?"
She's hungry. We're all so hungry. If I answer, does that
win me five points on The Fake Friendly Relationship
Scale? Maybe seven points if I tell her where I'm from?
Another five if I tell her what my parents did?

I'm so sorry, sweet, good nurses, but I don't know you. It's
work to make a new friend. It requires energy that I don't
have. I wish I did. I could use a new friend. But I'm too busy

taking in the plasma of two hundred-forty strangers, and who can even begin to count the number of their antibodies swimming into me.

These soldier antibodies, I need to help them out, tell them where to go and what to do, help them calm my looney, manic crew, perhaps distract them, perhaps seduce them. No one really seems to know for sure what they're doing in there.

And then one day a nurse comes and we are both so happy to be together and talking, and even have stuff in common. She's concerned about my symptoms. She tells me things that she says she's told nobody else. And I support her dreams.

She inserts an IV. And it doesn't hurt! And she doesn't need to try again. And again. And we giggle; and then I rest; and then we eat and laugh; and then I rest. And then after eight hours, she takes the needle out and goes home. And I sleep.

I only hope she'll come again.

DINNER PARTY

(I sit at the head of a large, impressive, oak dining table, with twelve formal, elegant place settings. And seated around the table with me are eleven clearly successful professionals:)

THE OPHTHALMOLOGIST who gave me the blood test that revealed my MG diagnosis, who later thought my sudden partial blindness was because I wasn't drinking enough water.

THE NEURO-OPHTHALMOLOGIST who thought the blindness might be the result of a few ministrokes.

THE TALL, HANDSOME DOCTOR, in his seventies, who wanted to put me on Retoxyn, and the MG SPECIALIST who thought that Cellcept would be better.

THE LIVER DOCTOR, a friend, who maybe because of caring about me as I anguished, "Should I go on Cellcept? Or Retoxin?" said, "Why don't you just start with the less aggressive drug?" Simple. Easy. Obvious.

THE BRILLIANT NEUROLOGIST who was good with data, but with too many patients to have time to check if she had the right chart before answering my questions online.

MY FIRST DOCTOR, who fired me because I got a second

opinion, and MY SECOND DOCTOR whose second opinion included calling my pharmacy to recommend his favorite drug, totally alienating MY FIRST DOCTOR.

THE NATUROPATH/MD who told me to take CBD oil four times a day, and THE NEUROMUSCULAR SPECIALIST who told me that CBD oil would be bad for my central nervous system.

MY OLD CATARACT SURGEON, whose remedy for my sudden double vision was, inexplicably, "Get a prescription for a new pair of glasses." Not that I had ever had a prescription for one.

(Everyone gets settled. And then there's a long, long pause. Finally, I speak:)

"I SUPPOSE YOU'RE WONDERING
WHY I'VE ASKED YOU ALL HERE."

Part IV. MARTHA GRAHAM,
INITIALS MG

MARTHA GRAHAM

Initials MG. Not only for Myasthenia gravis. For Martha Graham. The famous modern dancer and choreographer who changed the face of dance in Europe and America. The genius.

During my fifty years as an actress, I used to write her initials in my scripts as cues to summon any number of deep feelings -- awe, respect, passion. And on and on.

When I was three and a half, my mother sent me to the Martha Graham School of Contemporary Dance. "So you wouldn't become a klutz like I was," she said. Not understanding I only wanted to be like her.

Martha was my mother's hero. So she became mine. We worshipped her. Mother took me to every one of her Broadway shows, Martha starring in every single one. I will never forget her as Clytemnestra, the Greek warrior who murdered her husband because he'd killed their daughter. ("Gravis.")

When Martha came on stage, it was as if the sun showed up. As it was when she walked into one of her classes. Where maybe she punched somebody in the stomach to demonstrate her famous "contraction." A sudden sucking in the gut. She did it to me. Knocked the breath out of me. And it hurt.

When I was twelve, I was invited to take class with Martha's professional company. Mother and I were ecstatic. My father, however, threw and broke his chair one night at the dining room table, screaming, "No daughter of mine is going to be a dancer! I'll throw you out of the house!" And we lived on the seventeenth floor.

My mother was silent. I never took classes with the company. And that summer I was sent out of the country, probably as far away from Martha as Father could feasibly find. To Switzerland, no less, where I was not dancing. And mainly eating chocolate. And heartbroken. I put on forty pounds. When I returned to New York, I was convinced I was too fat to be seen at the school.

At college, one of my PE options was to take a dance class. I went. The beginning of the class included the same warm-ups I had done at the Graham School. And I ran out of the class, threw myself onto the ground, and sobbed into the grass as deeply and loudly as I think I have ever sobbed. The next week, I went back to class. But it was college, not a career.

Ultimately, I became an actress. (I lost the forty pounds.) I created a one-woman play for myself that got a rave review in *The New York Times*, and I was back at the Graham School taking classes. "Serious actors" took movement classes, singing lessons, fencing. It's a long list.

With the review, I had become a mini-star in New York, even starred on Broadway; and David Wood, my teacher at the Graham School, asked if I wanted to audition for the speaking role of Emily Dickenson in Martha's famous dance about the poet. For the company's upcoming Broadway season. And I would audition for Martha, herself.

Was he kidding? LIKE I WOULDN'T SAY YES?!! I auditioned. I got the job. I was invited to Martha's home for her to coach me. Every object there, breathtaking. Ancient artifacts. Sacred icons.

I read for her. She had one correction: at the end of every line, she wanted me to imagine the word AND. "The most important word in the English language," she said.

But it was 1970, Martha was eighty-seven, it was the first year she wouldn't be dancing. Her identity for decades. Her drinking got out of control and she was too drunk to teach me the dance. The original cast was brought in to see who could remember it and do the role. I was let go. I was heartbroken. Again.

Three years later, Martha was sober. AND, she

was choreographing. She asked me to read a poem for her new dance for the company's upcoming season. She was back on her feet.

And then she called to say that her good friend, the actress, Marion Seldes, was returning to New York and Martha wanted to work with <u>her</u>. I was heartbroken. Again.

Father stopped me dancing, and then Martha. I got knocked down, and then I got up. Again. And again.

And then I wrote two plays for myself to perform, both about women famous for their dancing. *Miriam's Dance*, and *Jane Avril*, about the Parisian cancan dancer who first danced the cancan like everyone else; and then, when she came to dance her own dance, she became a star.... Both were produced in New York.

And I danced.

A year ago, my Myasthenia gravis hobbled my walking, and paralyzed my arms. A year later, I can walk, I can lift my arms. Being occasionally short of breath doesn't mean I can't dance. I can. I do. I will. Dance.

Part V. DID THEY REALLY HAVE TO ADD
THE "GRAVIS??"

DID THEY REALLY HAVE TO
ADD THE "GRAVIS??"
It Didn't Sound Serious Enough Without It?

This "Gravis." From the Latin
or Old French.
Meaning Grief,
something heavy.
Grave. Really serious.
Good Grief.

******

I refuse to write here with Gravitas
(same root as "Gravis").
How could anyone digest it all?
Gotta throw in some jokes,
get all of us laughing
so when the Pill of Truth appears,
(never an easy pill to swallow)
our mouths are open
and we can just pop it right in.

******

I Gravitate towards smart people,
possibly my downfall,
so many are so left-brained

145

they can't think with their hearts,
and when I'm with them I feel
I can hardly stand up,
Gravity notwithstanding.

******

I do not have one foot in the Grave!
But these are Grave matters,
and some people with MG
end up in one before their time.
(Definitely "Gravis.")

******

Like Gravity, Myasthenia gravis holds me
down. But will not hold me down!

Instead, let me imitate the circus
clown able to align himself
with lines of Gravity so
he can balance on
a bright red
rubber ball,
on one finger,
upside down.
Upside
down.

******

Some of the words in this part of the book have the same root as "Gravis." Some don't. As the French say, "*Pas Grave.*" Meaning, "No big deal."

Sometimes I've included words that start only with "Gr," or even "G." And I've capitalized the "G's." So sue me. I Get carried away. I'm excavating for clarity in a snowstorm.

And if all of this is just silly nonsense, surely there's a lot to be said for silliness. Which is possibly as Good an antidote for MG as any of the medications my doctors have Given me.

******

A Graver is a sculptor.
And I must, now, re-sculpt my life,
must fashion exquisite statues
of a New Self.

No Graven images in gold,
but something more compelling, friendlier.
Flesh.

******

Gravis is also a wine.
From Gravis, France --

Dry red or dry white.

GIVE ME A GODDAM GLASS OF WINE!

Except I'm forbidden alcoholic beverages
WITH THE MEDICINES I'M TAKING!?

How Good could they be if they don't
let you Get drunk once in a while?!

Drunk! We must Get drunk! On poetry.
On art. On love.
On anything, we must Get drunk!

******

Grrrrr. I growl.
A mad dog
in fancy clothing.

******

"Myasthenia Kalon." Greek for
"Beautiful Myasthenia."
I could believe it was a beautiful
Greek island – with a lot of sun,
trees, and brightly colored flowers,
where I could walk on the beach,
feet in the warm water

(just the right temperature)
and I could feel calm, embraced, safe.
Not sick.
Not sick at all.

******

This MG is no fairy tale,
though the Brothers Grimm
were often Grim.

******

Grim, Grimmer.
Grimmest.
Grim Reaper.

******

I'm told to pick up Gravel from the road and keep some in my pockets in case the five coyotes in the neighborhood try to ambush me and my dog.

Presumably, I'd take the Graceful Gravel from my pockets and spray it out over the coyotes who would run. As if the stones were Grave portents.

Would my ambush by MG be as easy to make vanish.

******

I'm going to rhyme the word face
with the word Grimáce,
since the steroids distort the shape
of my once high cheekbones
and once expressive eyes.

I now have puffy cheeks, thinner skin,
the old imbalances, exaggerated.

Oh fuck it,
let me just make a clown face
and be done with it.

******

Sometimes Gruesome,
sometimes Gregarious,
sometimes silent,
sometimes Ghoulish,
MG, like a Grenade,
has blown up
what I thought my life
would be.

******

Did they really have to add the Giraffes?
I meant to write "Gravis." I wonder why
I wrote "Giraffes." Maybe because their legs

often splay because of how they're constructed;
and I sometimes feel like that (once invincible)
and then they can't get up, and then
they die. Or someone shoots them.

Or could it be the Giraffe's long neck,
my own long neck once considered
"a thing of Grace and beauty?"

I remember my second month with MG,
when my neck couldn't hold up my head.
How dare this MG have me endure
such an indignity as a floppy head?
Without a floppy hat!

******

"Gravis." It sure ain't Gravy.
It sure ain't Thanksgiving.
Don't got no turkey with stuffing,
no cranberry sauce.
No sweet potatoes with marshmallows.

Ain't nothing like Gravlax,
my favorite smoked salmon,
sugar and dill-cured.

"Cured..."

******

151

My newly Gravelly voice
pisses me off,
my throat muscles
tired, weak, stupid.

When I was an actress, I could be heard
in theaters that seated three thousand people.
Never used a mic.

My straining voice, now, is sometimes
barely audible from the disease –
(not only from my screaming,
silent, in the night, terrified
I can't hold up my head.
Or swallow).

******

This "Gravis."
Grist for the mill?

"Not by bread alone," of course,
but gimme a sandwich, some meat
between the slices. Leave the Gristle.
Find the meat that's tender.

Must put more tenderness in my life.
I can do it.

******

I love that the French use the word *"Grave"* colloquially
to mean a person who is crazy or an imbecile.

And in French slang, *"Grave,"* all on its own,
also means "Right on. Absolutely."

There's also what the French humorist,
Francis Blanche, observed:
"Quand on a la santé, c'est pas Grave d'être malade."
Meaning: "If you have your health,
it's no big deal if you get sick."

And fuck him.

******

No Green Room for me
in a Broadway theater.
Green tea can't fix it.
Nor Gregorian chants.
Nor Green hills. Nor Gargantuan
sticky, hot fudge sundaes.

******

Grrrrr. Yes, I'm angry.
My old life, a good life, gone --

maybe the new life –
better.

******

This is no Grendel monster
a Beowulf could kill.

They tell me my disease
is alive and with me
for the rest of my life.

******

This MG, a Grifter.
Greedy.
Smiles one minute,
robs the next.

I am forced to be
a Gambler.

******

I gave no Green light
for my immune system
to have a nervous breakdown,
and I can't find a therapist,

psychoanalyst, meditation guru,
reiki master, anybody,
to make it sane again.

******

I'm on the Griddle.
MG, this Waffle Man,
brands me with his heat.

But where are the Griddle cakes?
Must I only dream of pancakes
with blueberries and thick, sweet,
triple-whipped cream?

Then let me dream also of Greengage plums
(sweet and sour), Graham crackers, s'mores!
Gooseberries, Guavas! Grappa! Guacamole!
Gumbo! Gruyère on a baguette –
with lots and lots of butter.
And more butter.

Nothing "Gravis" about all that.

******

GROUNDS FOR DIVORCE.

Me and MG,

the marriage sucks.
I lose Ground.
Then, I advance.
Must stand my Ground.

Surely, it will be
Groundbreaking,
My New Identity.

******

Grrrrrrrrrr.
You! Ground squirrels!
Don't eat my roses!

******

Let me Gravitate towards joy, away from fear,
Towards jubilance, away from worry,
Towards laughter, instead of petulance,
Towards God, instead of towards myself.

******

I'll find the Groundwater.
I'll lay the Groundwork:
Diet! Medicines! Pleasures!
Be a Groupie for my healing,

not a Grouch. Won't Grovel,
won't Grind my teeth or Gripe,
won't hold a Grudge. Or surrender.

But be merry, not Grumpy,
not Gruff. And won't Grumble.
I'll Grow up and still create,
Grow old and out-Grow this MG.
Will surrender my old identity
but not my Joy.

Not my Joy.

******

Gravity: the force directing us – not just to any place on earth, but to its center. As if we were all seeking some Geometric confluence with the very center of the earth, not just the Ground under our feet.

How, then, best to honor the deep pulling of my body to the molten, metal sun at Earth's Center? I am hungry to feel balanced. Centered.

******

Accent Grave. That's French
for the slanting line on top of a vowel,

from high up left
to lower right.
How elegant is that!?

Climb up that mountain! Get to the top!
Sunlight! Views! Accomplishment!
No "Gravis" there.

∎

In English, the slanting line
in the other direction,
as in the word *belovéd*,

means "Put the accent here,"
or "Sound an extra syllable."

As in my challenge
to be my own
Belovéd.

******

MG is no relation to Graves' disease
although I'm sure my thyroid isn't happy,

and it surely has nothing to do
with the poet Robert Graves,

though here I am writing poems
to my MG.

******

Seeing me
with this disease,
would my Mother
turn over in her Grave?

How great would that be,
maybe she'd be back.
And make everything better.

******

A Gravitt is a pregnant woman,
and I am pregnant with questions, doubts,
worries, and anger big as a boat.
No wonder my stomach's as big as a melon.
I'm also about to give birth to this book.

And also to a new life.

******

A Gravitational lens is a cluster of Galaxies
creating a Gravitational field reflecting light
and refracting light, as we, too, all spin light
off of ourselves and maybe heal.

My mother wanted me to be a star.
All of us want to shine.

******

Myasthenia Gravis gives me
a new, illuminated self.

This is serious.
Grave.
The Gravy.
Of Grave importance.

Did they really have to add the "Gravis?"

YES.

Part VI. FINAL SONG
After 25 Months, and Feeling Much Better.
November 2, 2023 (My Real Birthday)

HAPPY BIRTHDAY TO YOU

Happy Birthday to You,
Happy birthday to me –
I feel so much better!
Now, how could this be?

'Cause I stopped taking Mestinon?
'Cause I started the Nattozyme?
'Cause I finished this memoir?
(Which took much too much time!)

And look, now I can see!
Not a patch, either eye!
Could the cause be the weather,
BECAUSE NO ONE KNOWS WHY!?

'Cause I left six good doctors
And I now have just one?
"Too many chefs!" said my doctor.
(Should I try having none?)

(For the following stanzas,
still and always to the tune of
"Happy Birthday to You.")

Was it all those surrenders?
Or the doctors, or the nurses?
Or my dog, or my diet,
Or this book and its verses?

Was it love from my friends,
Or electrons from Earthing?
No one knows, maybe only
'Twas the Time for Rebirthing….

Major symptoms are gone!
Did they just run their course?
Was it seeing my Immune System,
That formerly crazy horse?

'Cause its antibodies screamed,
"What we want is some steak!"
And I ate some, and felt better!
(Though they didn't want cake.)

Those smart antibodies called
For new Rules of the Game:
"Add more Love, Joy and Caring!
Do less Work! And fuck Fame!"

I don't know why I'm better,
Some of the above, all, or none?
Or the message from my antibodies:
"Go on out! Go have fun!"

Happy birthday to you!
Happy birthday to me!
It's the end of the book now,
May it be the end of MG!

AND MANY MORE!

MY THANKS

I'm getting better. The dosage of my steroids is down from thirty milligrams to five; my eight-hour immunoglobulin infusions are gone. I have more energy. As for my eyes, reading is still not always easy, but my seeing blurry, or double, is just about over. And let's face it, I even finished this book. For all this, I owe thanks to the following people:

MY DOCTORS. Heartfelt thanks go to my Ultimate Medical Triumvirate, without whom I know I wouldn't be so much better: Dr. William Buxton (Fastidious. Maverick); Dr. Carolyn Martin (Goes an Amazing Extra Mile); and Dr. Cynthia Watson (Smart. Thorough. Caring).

MY NURSES. A special and huge thank you to Charv Albano and Bernadette Foti, who separately came to my house to give me what seemed like endless infusions, nurses practicing nursing at a whole new healing and holistic level, of which I had never dreamed.

MY HOSPITAL VISITORS. Thank you, Antonia Bath (Wondrous. Prodigious!); Piers Bath (Loving); Lior Klein (Stalwart. Loyal); Peter Kazaras (Music Genius); Laura Owens (Generous. Loving); and Pam Shaw and Victor Talbot (Double Love Threat).

Inordinate thanks, too, to the woman who came into my room my first night in the hospital to neaten up. And a different woman who came to neaten up on the second night. They asked me if I believed in God? Yes. And then they called out, "God heal her!" and asked me to follow them with "God, heal me!" And again, and again. I don't remember their names, I was in shock and half-paralyzed, but I will never forget their compassion, passion, and heartfelt caring for my healing. Those two nights and those fifteen minutes gave me more hope than all twelve days and eleven nights in the hospital.

BACK HOME. My thanks to the neighbors who surprised me by cleaning out my fridge and cleaning up my house for my return from the hospital: Antonia Bath (Force of Nature); Marlene Frantz (Brilliant); Kelly Rockwell (Breathtaking on all Fronts).

WALKING. When I returned home, it was unsafe for me to walk alone. I wobbled; my balance was tenuous. Nonie Shore (Formidable Organizer) found me neighbors who would walk me and my dog: Charles Bernstein (Who Could Architect a Person's Life) and Barbara Webb (Kind. Supportive).

DRIVING. Back home, since my eyes would suddenly see blurry or double, it was anything but safe for me to drive. These neighbors volunteered to get me to my doctors– no charge: Carrie Armstrong (Talented. Stalwart); Richard Bowers (Generous); Ben, Sam and Nonie Shore (Adopt Me!); and Max Crawford, 19, who said he thought it was too sad anyone should have to pay anyone to drive them to a doctor. Which made me cry.

Thanks, too, to the drivers I paid: Jenise Blanc (Jolly. Caring); Randy Chance (Creative Encyclopedia); Michelle Elliot (With Kids); and Tiffany Pechinpauch (With Dog).

GETTING MY WORDS INTO THIS BOOK. Because my eyes had trouble seeing my computer clearly, or at all, I was mercifully able to dictate my hand-scribbled drafts to these brave, smart typists: Caleb Briskman (Diplomat); Sierra Friday (More!); Diana Mathur (A Talent and a Rock); Sam Shore (Magic); Micah Sohl (Tree and Horse Whisperer); and Allegra Torres (Joyful Factotum).

And for the final stretch: the shining, factotum/amanuensis/ doulas: Mia Altieri (Who Can Save a Person from Drowning); Trina Calderon (You Go, Girl!); Lauren Purves (Can Garden up a Document); Cera Studybaker (Healing the Planet); Aubrey Swander (Can Do Anything); and again, the endlessly gifted artist, Diana Mathur.

READERS, FRIENDS. With deepest gratitude, I thank and celebrate the following friends, to whom I have long trusted my books, not only for feedback, but also for the courage to put them out in the world: Yukiko Amaya (Transformational!); Jan Barry (Brave. Wise); Terry Belanger (Always); Richard Bellet and Sa Belle Sylvie (Five Thousand Miles Away, But They See Me Close); Jim Burroughs (Heroic Warrior); Rachel Chodorov (Artista!); Jo David (Advice Maven); Jack Heller (Consummate Man of the Theatre); Cathy Hull (Rembrandt. Clever); Neil Janovic (Amazing Multi-Support); Liza Lee (Cheer Leader Extraordinaire); Bonnie Loren (Inspirational!); Eileen Peterson (Generous. For So Long); Dr. Lisa Plymate (Such Good Council); Megan Rice (Strength and Support), whose dear, brave, and loving husband, Greg Humphries, has sadly just left us; Jimmy Roberts (Wise. Smart); Pamela Shaw (Artista Completa!); Jennifer Strom (First Class Writer. Dear, Dear Friend); Colston Villanueva (Consumate Acrobat); and Kellee White (Heart and Wisdom). I love you all.

Yes, it's a long list. A person who's sick needs a lot of help. I did. And with so many people willing to help, perhaps it is no surprise that I'm finally feeling so much better. I love and bless them all.

ABOUT JANE MARLA ROBBINS

PLAYWRIGHT. Commissioned by the Kennedy Center in Washington, DC to write and perform the one-woman play *Reminisces of Mozart by His Sister*, Jane also performed it at Lincoln Center in New York. Her first one-woman show, the OBIE-nominated *Dear Nobody*, which she co-authored with Terry Belanger, ran for a year off-Broadway, was produced on CBS, and toured to London and all over the United States. Her play, *A Radical Friendship*, about Martin Luther King, Jr. and Rabbi Abraham Heschel, was produced in New York and Los Angeles starring Ed Asner (available on YouTube, ninety-seven laughs in its one hundred and seven minutes, people leaving the theater crying).

POET. A Finalist for a Poetry Grant from the National Endowment of the Arts, Jane is the author of *Poems of COVID-19: The First Three Months*, a theatrical rendering of which is available on Instagram [@janemarlarobbins]. On YouTube, you can see her reading from her best-selling *Poems of the Laughing Buddha*, from her *Dogs in Topanga: 2000 – 2018*, and from her *Café Mimosa in Topanga*, winner, the 2018 Southern California Book Publicists' Poetry Award.

AUTHOR. Jane's best-selling self-help book, *Acting Techniques for Everyday Life: Look and Feel Self-Confident in Difficult Real-Life Situations*, and its accompanying flashcards, *Perform at Your Best: Acting Techniques for Business, Social, and Personal Success*, won the Gold Axium Business Book Award. Jane teaches the techniques at universities and corporations and coaches privately. She has also written essays for *The Los Angeles Times*.

ACTRESS. Film: *Rocky I, II, V, Arachnophobia.* Television: *ER, The Heidi Chronicles. Broadway: Richard III, Morning, Noon and Night.* Favorite roles: The Pet Shop Owner in the *Rocky* movies, and the Clown Ringmaster with *Circus Flora.*

For more information go to www.JaneMarlaRobbins.com.